MW01232752

THE
PAIN
INSIDE
MY WINDOW

The Road To Entrepreneurship

Author Sunrize Jackson

The Pain Inside My Window
The Road To Entrepreneurship
by Author Sunrize Jackson

Cover Design:
Editing: Gloria Palmer Walker

Contact the author at:
Email: sunrizeflavor@gmail.com
Facebook: Author Sunrize Jackson

Dedication and Acknowledgements

Dedication

To Mom and Dad, Earnestine and Coy Jackson, for instilling in me with the values of an entrepreneur.

Acknowledgements

Thank you to my mentors—Shawn, Swift and CJ— for all of your encouragement. Thank you to my right hands—Danielle and Amy—and the whole Visions Tax team.

Thank you to my daughters—Erica, Aaliyah, and Paress—who had to endure as many sacrifices as I did while I was pursuing my business, and thank you for sharing me with so many people who needed me.

Table of Contents

THE PAIN INSIDE MY WINDOW

The Road To Entrepreneurship

Chapter 1

I Was Born In This

As a child, my parents' main business was an upholstery business; my dad learned this profession long before I was born. He had a skill to make things beautiful—beautiful furniture—no matter where they lived, Los Angeles, Chicago, or all the way to Timbuktu. My mom and dad survived on their upholstery business. They would enter the customer's home, and I would sit and watch them measure furniture while the customer turned pages in the material books, trying to pick out colors that would match their home. My mom was great with the numbers and I would watch her write out estimates. As we went on each appointment, Dad would have my two older brothers help him stack the furniture on the truck, while Mom collected the down payment and service fees.

We were a middle-class family living on just the upholstery business, so when there were no customers, things would sometimes be pretty tight. I remember one night in the early seventies when our lights were turned off after returning from an out-of-town trip. Those were the sacrifices they made back then just to do a family vacation, but there was no way Daddy was going to let us stay in the home with no lights. So, we drove to the city and stayed in their upholstery shop located on the west side of Chicago where my mother grew up. My two brothers and I watched my dad work all night, upholstering a living room set he had found, while we ate from an electric plate and slept on cots.

By morning, Dad had the furniture finished and he sat that furniture set in the window of the store with a big smile that said he was proud of the work he had done with his hands. By noon, the furniture was sold. Most people don't understand the sacrifices a family makes when they are part of an entrepreneur's life.

Marketing Yourself

My mother, in her own way, taught us how to sell things. Sometimes marketing yourself comes at an early age. At age five, she taught me to set up a table and sell lemonade specifically to our neighborhood. Mom would get on me about getting out there and selling that lemonade. I was so shy that it took a whole week before I got my first sale. This was a little uncomfortable because we were the only black family in the neighborhood, and back then, there were maybe five black families in the suburb we lived in.

Being in business is no joke, and anyone who says it is a piece of cake possibly is not giving you a full perspective of what business is really like. Marketing yourself can take longer than you expected, and it may take days, weeks, or even months before you get that sale. Being an entrepreneur is work and it takes much determination and a lot of drive to carry it through.

As each day went by, Mom encouraged me to talk to people in our neighborhood so they would buy the lemonade. Day after day, however, I sat there with no intention of talking to anyone who passed by. Often in business, people think their product will sell itself, when in fact, it needs someone who knows the product backward and forward to sell it, talk about it, and uphold it as the best product ever. Somehow, we must learn to step out for that first sale.

My first sale came from a group of construction workers in the neighborhood who were looking for something to quench their thirst. After working hard, the first guy said, "Hey, buy her lemonade!" Mama said he was the foreman. After that, they all rushed in and the sales began. This lasted about two weeks while they were there doing a project. When their work was completed, they left. I learned I could make big sales if I waited until someone came into the neighborhood building something or pouring concrete, or somebody was performing work in the neighborhood. I walked around the neighborhood looking for people who were working hard and sweating. When they came into the neighborhood, I put up my stand and let them know that I had the BEST lemonade.

A lot of times in business, we forget to be ourselves and to be kind, gentle, and in control of our emotions, because sometimes, those emotions can make or break a business. I learned early to be **patient** in business. Sometimes the wait can take a long time before things really start moving. After waiting for weeks, the next thing I knew, all the construction workers were back and forth all day, buying my lemonade. That was the beginning of marketing myself. I fell in love with making my own money.

The best strategies must come early in the business. Your success depends on how well your sales or service goes. You can find yourself spending more money than you are making because you are afraid to step out and use your own voice when advertising. Spending more money than you are making increases losses, which could result in you losing or stopping your dream because you are not able to make money.

What was your dream for your business before you started? That vision is what will sell your product. People believe in the product because the creator or the person selling it showed them the qualities and outcome of having that product. I watched my parents dominate the upholstery business for years because of the quality of their work, and they were the only black upholstery business in that suburb of Wheeling, Illinois, after moving the business to that neighborhood from Chicago.

Learning To Make Money And Targeting Your Market

When I got older, I began to sell candy from our back door. By then, we had moved to Missouri, and my parents became just as popular with their upholstery business in a place where most African Americans at that time didn't even own a business as they had been in Illinois. Most of the businesses African Americans did own in that area were grocery stores, liquor stores, clubs, or juke joints. Our upholstery business was something unique and different, and there wasn't anyone doing it for miles around. I think if they had done a statistics report, they would have found there were no competitors for at least twenty miles.

Targeting is especially important. Finding a place you can service customers and a location that will help your business flourish is particularly important. In our small town, getting to the closest store in town would take fifteen minutes on foot. Momma and Daddy helped me set up a candy store. It kept the people in the neighborhood from having to make the long walk to the store in the sun. I sold candy, soda, freeze pops, and potato chips. My mother even had a distributor come to the house to sell me the products wholesale. I dealt with all types of kids and some adults. I even sold to kids who had a dislike for me from school, who really came make trouble or be a disgruntled customer, but it stayed on my mind to get that sale!

What I learned in the candy store was that you must always be professional. I figured, let me handle business first, before we get to the good part which was having to go ahead and fight them or in better terms just handle it.

These are the things we have to learn in business. Even though you know people will take you out of character and will treat you all kinds of ways, you still have to maintain a professional attitude. Learning that at an early age was good because it helped form me into someone who can handle all types of individuals and situations.

There will be ups and downs. When you don't have anyone to help run the business, you have to be there. With my candy store, there was no one to help, but sometimes my mom and dad would chip in. If I wasn't home or busy, they would go ahead and serve the person who had knocked on the door. My parents always did right by me with that candy store. They let me make decisions for it on my own: the products I wanted, the prices I wanted, and how I was going to sell it. Those are the things I learned at ages nine through fourteen. The candy store taught me the significance of many things, such as handling money, attitude, and customers.

When my friends came in, they would think I was going to give them something for free, or they would ask for a discount. I had to learn early that that would hurt me and that I would not have enough money to order more products. That is what we do in business today. We try to shortcut and give people discounts and/or give them all these extra things to help them. In return, it ends up hurting your business, and sometimes, it hurts so bad that you can't buy more product. If you can't buy more product, you end up running yourself out of business.

I also learned that you always put the business first. How many times have you heard people talk about this same situation? How many times have you given too many discounts?

I kept the candy store until I was a freshman in high school. I was able to save money to buy all kinds of neat stuff that my parents did not have to buy for me, including my school clothes. From there, I would throw parties and fashion shows, and because I was so in love with the movie *Sparkle*, I named one of my events Sparkle's Fashion Show and Dance, or Sparkle Presents. I always liked to be different and to stand out. When in business, being unique is important.

Every Day I'm Hustling

In my early high school life, it was only me at home. I babysat for other families and helped Mom and Dad with the upholstery business, stripping the furniture or helping them load or unload the truck. My brothers had graduated and moved on. One thing I learned growing up in the business was, if you wanted to work, you could work hard and get paid that same day, instead of waiting on a paycheck. I found out I could make money on my own. Every time I helped strip furniture, my mom and dad would pay me when I got done. Sometimes, a few of my friends would be there and wanted to make a few dollars, and we would help Mom and Dad strip furniture and spend our money at the store or the local carnivals in town.

If you look around, you can find many things you can do that will pay you right then and there. I learned from watching my mother that we must find the need. Once you find that, you will make money.

Chapter 2

Purpose (What Is My Plan?)

Approaching my last years before graduating, I never really knew what I was going to do once I graduated, but I knew I loved doing my own thing. During my high school years, I took shorthand, typing, and consumer math—things I learned to be able to work in an office setting. As fate had it, I got married in my senior year and I had a baby right before I walked across the stage. I took up office technology as a vocational trade to learn ledgers, balancing accounts, and computers.

I never really cared for working for other people, but my parents had showed me how to use what you had to get to what you needed to survive. It was hard with a husband who was also young to provide for the family. Having a new baby, it had not occurred to him that we needed to do more in order to get through. I worked odd jobs, like waitressing and packing corn, which paid me cash. While going through a training program, I finally landed a job as an office clerk at a government agriculture office. There I learned many skills.

I learned many things in my personal life too. My husband did not want to work. He stayed away from home, hanging out with his friends, cheating with other women, and the list goes on. When our noticeably-short marriage ended, I moved to

Milwaukee at the age of nineteen. I went to college there for a short time, but within a year, I went back home. I tried college once again and took up Criminology. Off and on, I had this big gap of just trying to figure out what I needed to be doing. I even rented a skating rink that was not being used. On Sundays, Mom and I would open it and charge the young people in the area to come in and skate. Mom sold the food and drinks, while I played the music. I was able to pay my bills with that until I could figure out my next move.

As I grew older, I needed a better income source. By age twenty-five, I had moved to Memphis and married my second husband. I began working in the office field to maintain an income and I went back to college, this time in Computer Information. As I worked at different companies, I learned how to conduct better business, customer service, to prepare documents, to type up documents, and accounts receivable and payable.

At the age of twenty-seven, I jumped at an opportunity to work seasonal for the Internal Revenue Service. My primary job was entering the paper returns into the system. I was in a department where most people owed taxes, so I would also apply their payments to their accounts. It was amazing how many people owed because of random mistakes they had made on their tax returns. All I kept wondering was, how can I help them? After so much time working there, I left. I participated in a tax preparation course which caught the eye of my then-manager Annette. The next tax season, I went to work for Jackson Hewitt.

Service And Performance = Passion

Annette knew off the top that she wanted me to work under her because she had watched me closely during the six-week course. She knew I was eager to learn and I already knew many of the major components, but then, I had to deal with my husband. He was a man who did not want his wife to work and he made it extremely hard for me to begin a career in the tax industry. I was worried about my relationship because sometimes when dealing with a client, I had to work over my shift servicing them. He had already fussed about me working at the Internal Revenue Service; then, here I went again with Jackson Hewitt. It was like a struggle for him to say yes. He just did not want me to work at all. He wanted a stay-at-home wife.

After my first thirty days, I became an assistant manager. The crazy part was they moved me to a Walmart location to fill in for a manager who had left and had not given the managers any indication of when they would return. I noticed off the top what the problems and issues were concerning that location, and what may have happened there and maybe the reason why the manager had not returned. I noticed there were not a lot of customers stopping and pursuing their tax situations, and the phones were not even ringing. There was no action at that location.

Quickly, I called my manager and told her to hurry to get me out of there! She called the district managers and told them she needed me, and I was sent back.

In those few weeks, I learned self-employment, capital gains, and itemizing. We had one customer come in who had just moved from Virginia. She was so pleased with the help she received from me that she gave us a large picnic. There was food of all kinds, all over, enough for everyone. From that day, I fell in love with taxes and helping people.

Your product should say a lot about you and what you have to offer. It shouldn't be anything you can't explain or talk about. It should come from the heart. That's why people speak about doing something you love—having passion about something makes your business even more unique. A lot of people start businesses just for the money, but when you have a passion for something, the reward is so much greater.

I was only making seven dollars an hour at Jackson Hewitt, but I loved it. I went home that day and told my then-husband how my day was. I even told him that I loved what I did, but his response was, "Isn't that just a seasonal thing?" I paused, and in my disappointment, I just switched the conversation. My husband worked a nine-to-five, most times twelve hours a day. At that time, I was pregnant with my now-nineteen-year-old daughter. I guess his reality was the income was not enough.

I learned the most incredible things to help my customers, and every day, I met great and interesting people. I finished that season out with the tax industry heavy on my mind and the impact it made. I was ready for more.

I remember while I was working for the Internal Revenue a guy who had started a tax business. I cannot remember his name, but he made an impression on me. I had watched how people stood in line all the way outside his office. Oh my gosh. Instead of getting my taxes done for free at the Internal Revenue, I jumped in line to get my taxes done there, just because this man had impacted me by watching his commercials and the things he was saying that were so down to earth. I think one of the sayings in the commercial was, "It's on like a pot of neck bones!" I mean they even had people flying helicopters in the commercial. I said right then and there, "That is what I want to do. I want to do this." The tax industry was all in my mind, especially after that first season with Jackson Hewitt.

The next year I switched over to Liberty Tax, and I followed my favorite supervisor Annette for two seasons. I worked evenings while pursuing my business degree; I already had achieved my Associate in Computer Information. I also had clients I had picked up from school and prepared their returns at home.

My husband still did not want me to work. He was so bent on me being a stay-at-home wife, but that situation was not working for me. I encouraged him to start our own tax business with his 401k, but he withdrew the money to invest in some get-rich-quick schemes instead, which panned out to be just that—schemes. All I could think was, he did not believe in me enough to invest in me. I began to pick myself up from the disappointment and work some temporary jobs to start saving. Not long after, our relationship could not go any further. We separated due to his need for me to be at home and didn't want to see me progress beyond a stay at home wife. I could not be that woman who was just going to sit there. Even my dad had a conversation with him and told him he had not raised me to be like that. They had raised me to get up and go get it. A go-getter.

I called my best friend and said, "I'm leaving."

She said, "Okay. Let me help you find a job." She also told me, "You know, my department is hiring. You can come here."

I called my dad and said, "Pops, can you drive me to Milwaukee?"

He said, "Yeah, we can go."

That is the kind of dad I had—always ready. My best friend made sure I had an interview scheduled on that Friday. We got in the car and drove out on Thursday, and as you already know, I got the job. When I came back, I told my husband I was leaving.

I moved to Milwaukee and started working in Human Resources for a local hospital with my best friend. My husband stayed in Memphis. As I worked full time at the hospital, I took a part-time job for another Liberty Tax franchisee. I began to train preparers in the off-season for Liberty, as well as maintain a supervisor's role. We serviced over twelve hundred people there for three years, and out of those twelve hundred people, I prepared the returns for eighty percent of them.

I kept looking at the fact that I was being paid only a little over a minimum wage during tax season, but I could have been making more if I had my own company. My best friend kept motivating me to start my own business. She just kept saying: You should start your own business. You should start your own business. You should start your own business.

The owner or Franchisee that I worked for at Liberty Tax decided to leave and sell the business back to corporate in my last year there. I pursued my interest in franchising and to possibly getting his store. My mom gave me part of the down payment and I cashed out my full 401k after being with the hospital for four years. I left for Virginia, where the corporate office was located, and began my research on being a franchisee. The classes and corporate representatives seemed to give me a good perspective of the business and how being a franchisee worked. I met the CEO, John Hewitt, and took a tour of the corporate headquarters. I flew home with a plan to go ahead and get started.

I thought, since I had been an employee for seven-plus years, that I would be entitled to the employee opportunity to franchise with one hundred percent financing. That was not true. I came home to an email and phone call that I needed to add at least 30,000 to begin. Still motivated by friends and family to start my own, I began to look for a space.

Let The Start-Up Begin

Starting out most times is not the way you pictured it would be. Sometimes you really must use what you've got to get what you want. I found a statistic that stated:

> *Across all elements of business capital (human, financial, social), there is evidence to indicate that given their immigrant background, foreign-born entrepreneurs are able to create their businesses with more business capital resources than African American entrepreneurs. This helps explain why African Americans, who lack a traditional immigration pathway and heritage, are experiencing slower entrepreneurial growth than other minorities. And while it is difficult to make comparisons within ethnic groups, a higher percentage of Asian and Hispanic business owners are immigrants as opposed to native-born, which is*

consistent with the apparent centrality of immigration to the entrepreneurial progress.

The historical experiences of African Americans with institutional and individual racism have created a culture of distrust within the Black community. The legacy of slavery, Jim Crow laws, and repeated civil rights violations have eroded the trust of African Americans in the government, U.S. institutions, and social interactions for over a century. And this lack of trust is also reinforced by the negative experiences African Americans have with financial institutions when unsuccessfully attempting to secure a business startup loan. Improving trust within the black community and cracking down on institutional discrimination is essential to building black social capital and producing more successful African American entrepreneurs. There are no simple or quick solutions to address the level of social distrust among African Americans because it has been cultivated over four centuries of contact with U.S. institutions. However, the area where there is the greatest potential is with respect to improving the relationship between black business owners and financial institutions. Black business owners are more likely to have shorter relationships with their primary financial institutions than other entrepreneurs. Firm lender relationships are built over time and involve consistent interaction. Small businesses with longer lender relationships are more likely to be extended a business loan and less likely to be credit constrained. Social capital, undoubtedly, plays a significant role in the entrepreneurial process. And when compared to Whites, African Americans and other minorities have less access to professional social capital networks that are the foundation for business development and expansion.

At the same time, immigrants of color can effectively translate the networks and resources that are established as a component of the immigration process into social capital. Foreign-born minority entrepreneurs start their businesses with more resources and foundational elements in place, such as economically-viable affective relational networks, a pattern of monetary assistance from remittances, and higher levels of social trust. Migration-based relational networks and remittances are not a component of the African American experience in contemporary America, and African Americans have among the lowest levels of social trust of any group in the nation; therefore, these resources are not available to African Americans, which helps explain why black-owned businesses are growing at a much slower rate than other minority-owned businesses.

https://www.cbcfinc.org/wp-content/uploads/2019/05/CPAR-Report-Black-Entrepreneurship-in-America.pdf, p. 20

Due to not having funding ability, I was able to take the money my mother gave me along with the money the money from the 401K and invested it into the software and computers. I found a space inside a big yellow warehouse building called an incubator. Definition of an incubator: *Office, industrial, or high-tech space usually owned or managed by a local government development board and intended to provide an economical and supportive environment for new business start-ups.* That is where it all started, in a not-so-great location.

It was hard to run my business in that building. I didn't have anywhere to put my signs and I had to use a doorbell for customers to let me know they were downstairs so I could let them in because we had no other way of knowing. The places I saw before the incubator were expensive and way over my budget. Back then, a business loan would not work for me because of a few things: credit, assets, collateral, etc.

I was taught long ago, "Make a way out of no way!"

There was no parking lot and we parked on the street. We used an elevator and the stairs to go back and forth to and from my new office space. I found a graphic designer who was starting off at the same time I was, and we helped each other. He made ground signs, logos, business cards, and flyers. I gave out my flyers to people I knew who were in business or who worked somewhere that they could refer me.

I started out my first year with my co-worker Danielle from Liberty Tax helping me, along with one assistant. That coworker from Liberty Tax stayed with me from the beginning to the end. A lot of people will come and go in your business, but if you ever find someone unique, who believes in you and your vision, keep them because they are someone who will support you to the end. A lot of people came by referrals and some by the flyers. The people in my then-small circle were telling people about me, but most of all, one of my friends, Avenel, was the bullhorn. In my first season, I serviced one hundred people. It was the start of something, but based on my budget, it was not going to be enough to take care of everything.

Chapter 3

Stepping Out On Faith

My mom kept telling me to let my full-time job go in order to run my business. Other people kept telling me not to let it go. I was worried that I was not going to have enough income if I let my full-time job go just like that. It was an extremely hard thing to do. I was worried about who was going to help me when I was short. That was a very scary move. I can remember my mom telling me, "Oh, I am going to help you. I am going to help you... Just step out!" I was asking myself, "What am I stepping out into?" I called it "no-man's land" and that means without any other income to depend on. It was the scariest decision I have ever made. I don't know when would have been the right time, but if I could do it all over again, I would have waited until I was a little bit more secure with my own finances. Of course, when the feeling hits you, you just STEP.

In the beginning, my mother would help offset my personal bills to help me, and through the off-season, I would contract some short-term positions to stay above water. While at those companies, I would implement some of their customer service trainings into my employee policies because I knew one day I would need them after being a human resource assistant. Adding a little flavor to my service goals, we wanted to make sure to educate our customers in understanding their options and refund status, which was overwhelming for us. In the beginning, it was so hard to manage so many incoming calls asking the same questions. A lot of people were unfamiliar with taxes and all they wanted to know was how much of a return were they receiving. I knew people were afraid to trust. They wanted some security. They wanted to be able to depend on someone for the answers.

In business, one of the biggest parts of your performance is knowing what the client or customer needs most. We adopted a fact sheet showing customers the answers to their frequently-asked questions and gave addresses and telephone numbers to check on their statuses, only able to handle calls back then one-by-one. We only could afford one phone line and it was hard during the season of 2007. At the end of the season, the whole roof caved in and damaged most of our equipment. We had to move.

My mom suggested I move to a storefront in a decent area. I found a storefront in a plaza located on Silver Spring. The lease stated I had to fix my own repairs, and not only that, the lease had CAM (Common Area Maintenance) fees. Back then, I had no idea what CAM was. If you don't know what CAM means, it means there is an extra fee you incur when you lease commercial property. For me, it meant I would be responsible at the end of the year for all outside improvements done to the area. Anything like concrete construction, redoing the parking lot, and property taxes—that's part of CAM.

Advertising is a must and we had no money to run any advertising. I could not afford the sign everyone else had for their shops in the plaza nor could I borrow from anyone or a bank. The sign for that building was over $1400 so I bought a banner instead. I did attract some customers by that banner, but word-of-mouth had my clientele up by seventy-five more clients in that next year.

Then I started a referral program the next year, in 2008, for customers referring three or more people. Even though I had a decent year, it still was not enough financially to get through the year. You see, my plan to beat competitors' prices and charge a lesser price than most was hard when I still had overhead. So, my personal life suffered because mostly everything I made was for the business. There still was personal rent, lights, and car payments due. There was no room for anything extra in my life.

Being an entrepreneur and wanting to date was hard because dating or being in a relationship was a struggle. The other person may not understand those things. They just look at it like, Oh, she or he has a business, so that means they have money. Or, he or she has it going on. Some even will say, you are supposed to be helping me do this or that. Then, when you ask for help or you say, "I might be short," or, "Can you handle the rent for the next three months?" That answer will be a "no" quite fast. My life transitioned based off people judging that I had money because I had a business, and there was nothing I could say to them to make them understand any different. And that was sad.

When you are an entrepreneur, you are focused on growing your business. You are not a nine-to-five, just sitting on someone's clock; you are in a different zone. It is almost a must to find someone who has some similarity and someone who can understand and believe in you, or else this road will get rough and you will stay to yourself.

When it came to marketing, I never had enough money to do any marketing. I would have to borrow from my mother. I had a boyfriend at the time who was generous enough to lend me the money for a short commercial or anything that helped with my advertising needs. Everything I did, to me, was on a low budget and it never was enough to really grab a substantial increase in clients. So, in the beginning, word-of-mouth was the best marketing tool I had. And, in the beginning, word-of-mouth was building my company.

I still had Avenel who brought the most referrals and send people all the time. That is where it truly began. Avenel knew a lot of people and those people knew people. As it turned out, she really believed in me and was one of my biggest supporters. A lot of people in business say their friends and family do not support them. I hear that so much in business, but it is not even that. Sometimes it is the person behind them or someone attached to them who is sending people to you. Like, "I know her; go to her." That key person was someone who really helped my word-of-mouth advertising. Find you an Avenel for your word-of-mouth.

After my second year, we added another employee and we moved right next to a check cashing place. It made it very convenient that our clients could get the fast refund, get their check immediately, or if they wanted the loan or the fast money, they could just go right next door, which was awesome. The system was working and everything was going well. Then, suddenly, at the end of the year, the landlord comes and says, "Um... I would like for you to move."

I asked, "Why?"

"Oh, because I got a better offer and I'm going to move you to another place. Check your lease!" he said dominantly.

I said, "What?"

"Yeah. Your lease says I can do that. I have another space too I can send you." He replied.

See, most of us entrepreneurs, we do not check the fine print on things. Then, this man, who was rich as all outdoors, comes and says, "You've got to move." And I'm looking like, "What?!" But you know my mother raised me differently. She raised me to be not only tough but to emerge out of any situation with knowledge. I did not take his word. I took my lease to a lawyer to see if everything he had said was true. If the landlord was right, then I wanted to know was there anything I could do to keep from moving. After the lawyer looked it over, and this and that, he said, "What is the problem now?"

Can you imagine the look on my face? "What do you mean, what's the problem? I've got to move all my client files. I must inform them that I am once again moving. Not to mention, we are almost into a new tax year."

This would be extremely hard for me to pull off and was extremely uncomfortable for me. I was going to fail as he wanted me to fail. The lawyer had little to say other than the fact that I needed to pay his retainer. You find out in business as well as in your personal life that some people are not for you; they are strictly thinking about what is good for them. After a lot of thought, all I could see was, if I cut out of the lease or just went somewhere else, I would still owe the balance of the lease. I still would owe them all that money. I was stuck in a bad place, so I stayed and moved to where he'd asked me to move.

This move was a struggle. I had to find ways to call all of our clients. I had to send out emails and letters to notify every one of the changes. Me being on a very small budget, I had to deal with occupancies, signage, and marketing all over again. I hired two additional guys who were recommended by a friend. These two guys were smart and quite easy to train. They helped in the marketing by frequently spreading flyers throughout the city and they knew a lot of people. I paid them for distributing flyers by offering commissions. Having these two guys brought in double the clientele in the next season.

Plus, with Avenel's help from the previous year, I had the people I'd serviced the year before referring families. Those families had families, and we grew with them as well. But the internal problems with employee issues, which resulted in people coming to work when they wanted to come, or they had this problem or that problem, kept us from being available as much as we should have been. We dealt with that too often.

Chapter 4

Dealing With Customer Issues, Complaints, and Setbacks

We also dealt with issues with the clients and their attitudes. I believed some of them thought, that because we are black, we weren't doing everything right. Sometimes, they would have the "wrong" person bring them, someone they did not want to know any of their business, so they would not want to sit and give or get the information needed because they were trying to be discreet. We'd think, *'You brought them. Isn't that something?'* If they did not receive everything they needed, we still were blamed.

One time, we even had sisters fighting. One woman had her taxes done and brought her sister with her to pick up her check. The sister knew what the woman was getting and they began arguing about who owed what; then they began fighting. I knew, if they hadn't been in a black establishment or if they had been in a big franchise tax office, that normally wouldn't have happened. Those types of things made me realize that our company was not recognized or even considered with respect. I had gotten to a place where I did not want to deal with people anymore when it came to money. People are terrible when it comes to money, and their attitudes and their rush to get their money took a lot of patience. They were impatient because they wanted to take care of a bill with the money, or they were just mad at something that had nothing to do with us. I really wanted to come out of the industry with the way I was feeling.

I decided to get some fresh air and clear my head, so I partied all night on Valentine's Day in 2010, and I said, "This is my last season with this tax stuff. I cannot do it anymore. I am tired of this, all this dysfunctional stuff." I drove home exhausted, tired and stressed. I was so upset with my clients and the things that were going on, and I did not really have a personal life. I told myself the first thing I was going to do when I got home was start working towards getting out of this business.

On my way home, I must have fallen asleep or something of that nature. A city bus collided into me! I woke up and I knew God was in the plan. Oh, He was there! My leg was broken. My hip was broken. My ribs were broken. And, on top of all that when the ambulance came, I had a stroke. I had all of that going on before I came back to myself. Once I got to the hospital and they found out all that was going on and what all I was needing, everybody was saying little stuff out in the waiting room: "She isn't going to have a business anymore." Or, "She isn't going to be able to do such and such anymore." And another naysayer said, "She isn't going to be able to ride motorcycles anymore." They had what was going to happen to me all worked out. They just knew I was done.

After a few days, I had surgery. My oldest daughter at the time was eighteen years old. She stopped what she was doing to help her mother and jumped in the office. Along with Danielle, those two guys I told you about, and another woman, my daughter was trying to print checks and she called me early one morning.

She said, "Ma, I know you do not want to do it. And I know you are in the hospital and probably not thinking straight, but you've got a whole line of people waiting to pick up checks and they are hanging all the way out the door."

I paused for a minute to think hard and said to myself, "What am I going to do?"

She said, "Don't worry, Mama, and don't get upset. Just walk me through how you get into your computer and help me get these checks printed for your clients. Danielle will be here shortly, and we'll finish it up."

I said, "Oh man, I don't know how to do that. I cannot think like that."

My thoughts weren't where they were supposed to be. I barely knew who the president was at the time, you know, because of the stroke. I closed my eyes and thought hard. I began to go into work mode and remembered how to instruct her and began walking her through the process by saying, Open such and such, close that. Okay, now click on here and go down to something to that right there. Choose this. The next thing I knew she was printing checks. I could not remember a lot of things, but most of the things I could remember were about the business.

That was Visions Tax.

Chapter 5

The People Who Believed In You Vs. The People Who Doubted You

A lot of people came to visit while I was in the hospital. Several people said, "I don't want to see you like that, so I don't want to come up there." You get to the point where you think about all the people you have helped and things like that along the way, and you find out there are only a few who really love you and really have your back. Outside of my family and best friend, one of those people was Danielle.

Danielle is one of those whom I am going to tell you right now: Get yourself a Danielle! If you do not have a Danielle in your business, you will not make it. Danielle is one of those people who believes in your vision. I will say this again: "*Believes in your vision*." You can tell a few people about your vision, and you can even tell your family and friends about your vision, but they will not react to it. However, you will find that *one* person who will react and want to help you. They will want to see you win, and having myself a Danielle, I am grateful for how she stepped in at the times she has. How many of you have a person like that? If you do not, you need to find one. You will need them to help your vision become reality. She went over and beyond and stepped in while I was in the hospital and covered all my roles and responsibilities.

After I was released from the hospital, I was not able to walk for some time. I began to get around the office by wheelchair, then eventually, as I began to get stronger, I went by crutches. No matter what, I still had to go in to work. I still had to maintain that office. Not many people can do that. Under those circumstances, most would have let it go. I could not afford to do that. Danielle would keep the payroll going, and I would sign the checks for the employees. She made sure things were still running smooth.

Of course, I had my mom too. She made sure the rent at the office was paid and things like that. My boyfriend at the time made sure the rent was paid at the house. Even though I found out he was seeing *Sally Sue*, I didn't mention it at the time. I said to myself, "Just be quiet because you need help and he wants to help you." So, I decided to stay quiet.

It was crazy because my mom had promised to buy me a car. She had said, "Don't worry about your car; I'll buy you another one." I said, "Okay, Mom; thank you. Appreciate it." But it did not happen. You cannot always depend on people for things. People have other things that may come up or something else that is going on. When I came back and said, "I found something," she said, "How much money do you have? I'm sure you made something at the office."

People worry about what you are doing, how much you are making, what you are doing with your money, and those types of things. What they don't seem to realize is you have expenses. I was not able to be in the office for the whole month of February until the end of March. Not to mention, I was not walking. I was spending money when my employees' hours shot up because I was not there. All the profit went to payroll, but people did not see that. They are on the outside looking in and think that you have it! I was like, "Just forget it. I will figure it out and buy the car myself."

For the first time in my life I had to depend on people and some of them were the same ones who depended on me. I was used to my independence and it was gone. The crazy part was my boyfriend was so happy that I had to depend on him for different things. He would leave me in the house for days and I did not have a way to go anywhere, especially the office. I had to stoop down and ask my child's father to take me to get the truck I wanted to purchase. He took me to the auto dealer's, and he was nice enough to drive it and made sure it was securely parked.

From then on, if I needed somebody to take me somewhere, they would have to come and take me where I needed to go. That is the thing about your drive: You have to have the drive to be ambitious. Your ambitiousness sometimes must be so strong that you will be able to push through the things you never thought you could. This crisis I was in was one of them.

On the first day I was able to use my crutches to get in the car and drive to work, here comes Avenel, my best client of word-of-mouth referrals, who walked right in with a face that said she was happy to see me. She was proud. She looked at me and said, "You know everyone thought you weren't going to make it. They counted you out. They were saying, 'She isn't going to make it and what are we going to do as far as our taxes?' I told them, 'YES, she will!' I told them you were going to make it. They didn't believe in you, but I did. Here you are, and you got a new car already. No one is even in the office yet, but you pulled up in here and you made it to work anyway on crutches!"

I began to look at her in disbelief because I had never seen her so excited. I asked, "Are you all right?"

She said, "YES, I am fine."

That made my day. When I was at my lowest, here came someone who thought so much of me and told me something I needed to hear which helped me to move on. I was really at that place where I was doubting myself and doubting my capabilities. I pretty much was doubting everything going on. But, this one person—and please do not forget, this was my main marketing word-of-mouth person I told you about earlier—came when I needed to hear that.

I thought about my overhead and about my losses. I thought about everything that had happened that year. I talked to that landlord and I was almost out of that lease due to my situation, but I was not closed. I looked at my circumstances and thought, '*There is no way I can pay these prices, pay this type of rent, pay this payroll plus other expenses with the losses I've taken.'* I asked the landlord for a payment plan for the amount owed plus the remaining time of the lease so I could break it and move to a space I could rent that was much less. Sometimes people do not think about that either. If you want to get out of a lease, maybe you can negotiate something so you can move on. You may be able to plan out a better strategy for the next place where you can see a profit.

Imagine all the people around me who got paid: employees got paid, landlord got paid, contractors got paid. Everyone got paid—but me. So, basically, I was working for that landlord and giving him a pretty large portion of the profit.

Next, I went and found a place with low rent and overhead, an older building which didn't look like much from the outside but inside were people like me: people who were trying to get their businesses off the ground to a point where we could be comfortable. A barbershop, a beauty shop, an insurance agent, and a convenience store on the bottom. All were hungry to work hard to get to the next level. We made that building look good, seeing that it was run down a lot; we added a lot of flavor to it.

The landlord was a genuine old man, a really good old man. He had said, "I already own this building. I'm able to cut back something here and there if you run into a situation, or things like that." Plus, the lights and utilities were included. These are some things we as entrepreneurs need to look at when we are trying to find a property or space to rent. We have to think about those components because they are going to matter when you are trying to produce and have to shell out all these different expenses to keep your business going and to move up.

I made a couple of changes and changed my business over from a sole proprietor entity to a corporate entity, in case something happened that was detrimental, like that accident I was in or a crisis such as that. Then maybe I could keep the business in the hands of my team, or my daughters could pick it up and keep it going.

I still was thinking that my vision to be successful. Visions Tax meant so much to me, and in a way, the reason why I named it Visions Tax was because I would see that people had visions of their own: what they wanted to do with their tax refund and the changes they wanted to make in their lives. I would ask them, "What do you want to do with your tax refund?" I wanted to know and be a part of the vision of what they wanted to do with their money. That is where the visions in Visions Tax came from.

Chapter 6

Personal Relationships and Growth

Once I began walking, healing, and getting back into my personal life, the boyfriend I had at the time finally showed his true colors. He left as he would always do right after the tax season. I didn't know what was going on, but my friends and some of my family could see how he came and went. He'd come in right before tax time, and when he figured tax time was over, he'd find something to be mad about and try to leave me hanging. I guess he thought I was going to struggle because the tax season was over. I didn't give much attention to it because my goal and my mind were always set on my business. I never had time, really, for a true relationship.

When the next season came in, I was at a place where I was more secure. I now had an office I could afford, new clients to service within my building, and a new employee. This new employee, a biker sister of mine named Amy, also became a key component, and when I say, "key component"... I do not know if Amy saw the vision, but I know Amy believed in me. After the accident, she asked, "Hey; you okay?" Previously, she had said she knew I was going to need help in the next year, so she came through and started that year. Not only did she come, she brought her clients from the tax office where she had worked before. Amy had over seventy-five clients.

These are the things you must think about when you try to partner with someone or bring somebody in when you are building a business. You have to find those key components. Those key components will help you build your brand and your business. I added these two women (Avenal and Amy) and they never did anything outside of the business for a long time. My knowing that these two women always asked me first and they never gave approval to people without talking to me first was a unique thing. These women probably thought they were just as good as me with taxes or anything like that, but they never tried to take over or made a decision without talking to me first. These are the qualities you must find when you are building a team because it benefits your business and it reflects on you. Anything and everything you do will be shown. Amy came in and brought these clients with her, and we were able to pick it up and run with it.

Adding Amy's clientele, we inherited more hard-to-deal-with clients to the batch, but we liked the challenges and we made it work. I started getting clients who owed a lot of money—businesses and people who were already in trouble with different government agencies—and things like that; people who had businesses taking off and they needed direction. The dynamics of the services I offered began to shift. My focus started turning to that of a consultant, where my services would not necessarily stop after the tax season ended. I began to work throughout the year because those extra services needed to be offered.

It was funny to me because a lot of people use to ask why I wasn't adding other services when I first started the business, and I remember one saying, "Why don't you start an insurance company within your business?" Or, why don't you add this to your business or that to your business? I would say, "Let me master this one first." Yeah, you have to master it. You cannot lie: Yeah, I am going to do this or I am going to do that. People always say I am going to do something but have fifteen things going on they are trying to do and cannot accomplish even one.

Try to master that *one* thing, so people can say, I know she/he can do this. Since she already has my information, let her continue to help me on that because I already trust her with the first thing. That is what I was mastering: TRUST.

People do not know what you are thinking, but they think they know you. They think their suggestions are valid and you should use everything they are saying, but you are walking out your own vision and pushing this business the way you see it. Do not forget it.

The 2011 tax season had officially begun. We were into our 6th year and we were finally at a point where we were making a profit. It wasn't a big profit, but it was profit enough to maybe get through the year. That was my main goal: to get through the year. If I could get through the year, that was good enough for me. I knew if I had to, I would take my tax refund, pay up some things, and make it work.

There are a lot of people in business with problems because they do not understand how to budget their finances very well. A lot of people are big buyers, but I was never a big buyer. There were a lot of nice things I liked too, but I was going to wait until it was good for me. You must train yourself to wait for it. That was who I was. I never forget the hard times, and I remember where I started with Mama and Daddy in the back of that store. I already knew there could be ups and downs, slips and trips and tries, and things like that.

My mom would come to me and say, "Why do you like this tax stuff? It isn't making money as fast as it should!" At this time, Mama had a group home and was making close to a million dollars a year. She was doing good and doing big things with the group home, but by 2011, she was messed up with IRS because of payroll. Years prior to that, I had offered to bid on doing her payroll, both Danielle and I. I reminded her that Danielle had gone to school for accounting and payroll, and remember, I went to school for business. I was like, "Mom, this will give us an opportunity to really show what we can do if you give us the opportunity to do your payroll. Plus, we can get out of some of the stuff we go through during the off-season." Momma decided against it and went with someone else she felt was more seasoned. I was hurt, but it made me strong to realize that people must do what *they* feel is best for their business. There are going to be some letdowns, some put downs, and some people who just do not see or valuer your worth.

That situation with the IRS that came that year, came with a blow and I knew it was going to happen eventually, but I did not know it was going to happen so fast. Here she was, flying off the handle, saying, I've been helping you, and this and that, and you never have time to help me. The only thing you guys have time for is your customers or clients. You do not have time for me.

I was like, "Mommy, you didn't tell me anything about you needing help. In fact, you told me you didn't need me and Danielle to help you with your payroll."

She had sent me some documentation from the IRS stating she owed over one hundred sixty thousand dollars. I was like, "Oh my God... This has got to be an error!" I flew down there in a wheelchair because at the time I still could not walk far or long distances, but it was my mother and I felt I owed her everything to fix it. I jumped on her paperwork immediately when I arrived! I said, "Let me read everything."

After going through her paperwork, I noticed a receipt where she had obtained a lawyer, a tax lawyer, to get her out of the situation. I did not know anything about it. I was just going through the paperwork and found out that was what she had done. Plus, she had paid the lawyer seven thousand dollars. I looked through the paperwork and said, "It's talking about 941's and your payroll stuff, Mom. This does not have anything to do with taxes, as far as a regular tax return, at all." Because, of course, I was doing her tax returns, and you know, this is what people do on a regular basis: blame someone else. They blame you for stuff you had no idea about, knew absolutely nothing about—especially if they can blame you and still look good without taking any responsibility.

The first thing she said was, "That's my money. I can do what I want to do with my money!" At the time I was offended because I didn't understand. "What is she talking about?" We think everyone is on our level of understanding and that really messed me up. I thought, *'What is she talking about? That is not her money!'* Finally, I asked, "What do you mean?" She thought it was her money because she had paid the employees and all of what was left was hers. She didn't realize, that once you paid employees, a certain amount has to be paid to the IRS and the state for their taxes. That was the portion that was not being paid. It had added up over time to that large amount.

I said, "Give me your bank statements and all of your canceled checks. I will add them up and build a database for you. That will show the original amount you owe and the parts you have paid. Maybe that is why it is not being calculated outright." She gave me those items, and we dug until we found all the deficiencies. I was tired, walking on a cane, and trying to help as much as I could. Once I found everything and created a database of the payments that had been made, I asked for the agent's name who was giving her the most problems. We got on the phone and requested an advocate for Mom.

I put a whole package together for them. I said, "You know you've already gone into her accounts and levied her." They had even put a lien on her payments coming in from the State and it was costing her business tremendously. She did not have enough money to pay the employees she had on staff.

I said, "Ma, this *is* your money, but you have to understand, once you pay your employees, they have taxes too that have to be paid. That's what payroll service companies do; they take care of that. That is what you pay them for." What had happened was the payroll guy would give her a slip for her to mail the taxes from the payroll in herself. Sometimes she mailed it in when she felt like it, and like a lot of us, with so many bills and different things going in and out, we go, "I'll take care of this later."

My mom did not play any games and I give her credit because my mother never graduated from a college or business school. She was just super smart in everything she did. Imagine that she went from an upholstery business and preparing estimates, to running a group home. Her skill was taking care of mentally-challenged people. She was the best at that and mastered it. In that group home, those numbers and the things that came with it were big to manage.

Sometimes, when you are running a business, you are great at just the skill of whatever service you are providing, but not the administration and other things you have to do in order to operate it. That's why it's important to have a team who can help with the things you don't understand. They have mastered those unique things that will keep your business going. I had offered to be a part of that team a couple of years prior to that situation. Danielle and I were starving in the off-season and needed the work, but my mother's company had chosen someone else. After everything happened, however, I was the one who ended up having to fix the problems in the end.

I read that paperwork and realized, after I'd found everything and calculated it, that she really owed them about sixty grand. I had found all her payments and documented them for her advocate. Then I got another packet ready for her lawyer. I did all the work, which was much better than the work her lawyer had done. I was grateful, because when I needed Mom, she always came through. It was the best I could do for my family. Please remember, some family members may not value you like your clients do, but don't let it beat you down. They don't understand how to separate being a client from being family. That is one of the hardest things for them. But, in time if you work with them long enough, they will.

When the IRS agent actually came out to Mom's house, she saw all the documentation and everything, and said, "Who helped you with this bookkeeping?" Mom said, "That was my daughter. She does taxes." The agent said, "That's who you need to keep." I think that made my whole day, because after all those years, I do not think my mom really knew my value or why I wanted to go into the tax industry. I think that was when my mom finally saw the value of what I offered.

I remember when I first got into taxes, Mom was like, "What in the world? Why did you go into that?" And remember, my ex-husband did not understand it either. You may ask, "Why is that? Why don't they understand?" I believe they didn't recognize the value of my services and needed proof of my abilities. I now had more than just a few people valuing my service, I had my family.

After I helped Momma, the door began to open for me to help a lot of clients who had businesses with key things that were hurting their businesses. Most were keeping their documentation, expenses, and employee laws straight. With my HR experience, I was consulting on employee issues, IRS issues, helping startup businesses with choosing entities, and still sending clients to Danielle for payroll services.

➤✳︎◄

Visions Tax had begun to rise. I was still having friction with marketing. It was a major factor in my business, because by the time marketing came into play at the end of the year, I didn't have quite enough money to really do some of the bigger things some of the competitors were doing. I began to take out pawn loans. The first thing I pawned was my motorcycle. I frequently go back to a verse in the Bible, Corinthians 13:11: *When I was a child, I spake as a child, I understood as a child, I thought as a child: but when I became a man, I put away childish things (KJV).* That is when you realize you need to be more about your business and more about your family.

I honestly believe Visions Tax was given to me by my Father, God, and I began to say, "You know what? I am going to have to let it go." So, I pawned my bike, with hopes of getting it back, because I wanted enough money to have decent advertising, software, and those types of things. Plus, in the off-season, I needed to pay rent. Once the season started, I thought I would make the money to go get the motorcycle back. I thought it was a great plan.

Those people I used to pawn my bike to I thought were good people, but they had many complaints from other bikers that they weren't so nice. I never thought it would happen to me, because we got along so well, yet they got me right in the bucket, along with the rest of the people they did wrong. When I went back to get my biker or when I asked, "What's the total amount owed?", it was much different from what we had agreed on. I did not know why it had changed. I said, "You know what? I give it up." I gave my motorcycle up. The two things I loved most, besides my kids, were my motorcycle and my business; those two things kept me going. I sacrificed my motorcycle for my business. It was a setback, but I took the hit.

Chapter 7

A Seed is Planted: Partnering With The Right People

During the same year, I also took another hit because I had decided to open another location, two offices versus one, and the second office had been broken into. They stole the computers and all the little gadgets that came with them. However, they didn't touch the files. They also took the TV, VCR, and the surround sound system. That was the second loss and setback. To everyone else it seemed minor, but the expenses behind it—like the money used for rent, payroll, and commercials to advertise that location alone—were a gigantic loss.

I lost. I accepted that I had taken a big hit. I lost the motorcycle, I lost that location, and I lost a lot of profit. We have to realize that these things will occur, and we need to realize it is a priority to purchase business insurance. You never know when something like that will happen. I was glad I had and was able to replace some of the things, but I still had to pay off whatever I owed on other items, such as the lease and things like that.

I was once again back to one location. You must know when you are not wanted in a location. The break-in gave me an indication that I was not wanted nor were my services. Some people stay, that's on them, but I already had one office that was still choo-choo-chooing away, so I figured I'd chop my losses and gain it back later. As a risk taker, you have to be willing to go through a stumble or two, and a risk taker I am. I knew I had to keep fighting to keep my vision alive.

A year or so after that, the old man at the first building got sick. Yeah, he got sick, and two of his kids came in and began to take over and make some changes. I did not think I would like it and at first they began to show up in our offices and to show other people how nice our businesses looked so they could rent out the spaces that were vacant. I knew I had done a lot of work because we were in a building that was not the best. I had put a lot into it, all the way down to the carpet; plus, we had painted. We had done a lot to set ourselves out as different. That was my goal all the time. I always tried to make things a little bit different, make them better, and make it comfortable. My whole goal is service. If you don't put your passion in your business, then what are you putting in it?

Finally, my advertising was beginning to make sense with some of the businesses I had begun networking with along the way. Some of my advertising needs were worked out with payment plans. Some trusted me enough to wait until the season actually kicked in to receive their payment. Things were starting to look up. I even did a billboard or two, but ironically, no one who walked in said they had come because of the billboards. No one came because of any of the commercials. No one really came because of the flyers, but we still put those out. It was all about branding. It is important to get the name of your business ringing around, so by the time they hear it through word-of-mouth, they are ready to come to you. I even did a little radio advertisement. In the end, the best results were from word-of-mouth. Word-of-mouth is people saying you provide a service that they liked. So, once your advertisement is out and people are giving testimony of your services, the people WILL come.

The other services I provided began to kick in at a steady pace. I began to look around at the area where my business was located and finally I was ready to relocate it so I told myself, "I'm going to get out of here." I had one client who was more to me than a just a client. We would talk about our businesses and use each other's ideas, and sometimes make suggestions. He was like, "You know what? This don't look like you." He said he had bragged about my services and everything I could do, "This building doesn't represent you. When you pull up to this building, I bet your customers are saying, 'Wow. Are we sure she's in here?' When you come outside, you have people hanging out on the sidewalk and nowhere to park. I'm sure that's scary to your clients."

I understood, but I also saw traffic and potential clients. When I looked outside, I saw people going into the convenience store, going downstairs to the barbershop or beauty shop upstairs, things like that. That was good traffic to me. I could not grasp what he was saying because these were my people who looked like me. That was what I said to him. As far as the building was concerned, yes, it could have been better. I had already had a few higher-end clients tell me they were a little disturbed by the outside and the people who hung out front. When you talk about money or anything concerning money, you do not want to be somewhere that seems to be dysfunctional. You want to be somewhere that shows who you are and the type of business you represent. Once again, after four years, I decided to relocate and upgrade to be able to service anyone, not just my people.

I found an office with a great look, and when I moved this time, I checked the lease and confirmed there was no CAM and that this lease was straight rent. All you paid was your own utilities. It was a nice-looking plaza in a pretty decent area. There were apartment complexes surrounding it and also the expressway was almost right in front of it. This was a great location. I was able to hold meetings and workshops, including self-employment workshops, to help people to understand and keep up with their expenses. That was especially important to me, because after Mama's crisis, I really wanted people to know more about what they were getting involved in. This was not something they could just play with, but most of them did, just like Mama.

I decided to partner with two businesses to help my clients with, "What are you going to do with your refund?" One was a dealership to help clients get into cars with their refund, and one was a guy I met through a colleague of mine who had credit repair services built into his business. He offered a package which had many other unique programs with it, but credit repair was one of the biggest things I wanted for my clients. I thought, *'I will partner with this guy, and this will help a lot of my clients with their credit issues.'*

Once the season began, some of my clients wanted me to take the money out of their tax return for the package they chose. Others paid upfront. I even got paid for my package. I wanted to at least try the product along with my clients to make sure they were receiving good service. He would come into my city, and we started doing events to help spread our businesses and the concept of the package he offered. I would also go with him to events out of town.

I watched him closely with his product and how he gained more people offering the packages. My goal was to learn more strategies in marketing because he was a very smart guy and he prided himself on marketing. Something I was not good at was getting on stage and talking to a lot of people at one time. He was very great at it, and I saw him reach many people, which resulted in him branding his business by just talking about it.

Six months later, my credit score had started moving, but I began to receive calls from my clients about theirs. They complained that nothing was happening to their credit. I immediately called him and asked, "Do you have somebody working on my clients' credit?" He responded, "Yes, they are being worked on." I started going down the list and calling all my clients who had purchased the credit repair package, and it seemed the only person who had received any help was me. I said to him, "You know you are the face of the company and you do not want this to be a problem." He explained to me that he had people who were working on all these things in the background. Long story short, I found out he wasn't fixing my clients' credit.

Meanwhile, on the other partnership with the dealership, our satellite office within their store actually did pull clients for me as well as give them the advances they needed to purchase vehicles. However, some clients still were dissatisfied and the dealership was worried about possible defaults from some of these clients. It is so important to partner with the right businesses. It takes some time to get use to it, and my main goal was always the satisfaction of my clients, especially if they trusted my judgement in doing business with any business to which we referred them.

By the next tax season, I had to take the money my clients had paid for credit repair in that year and give it back to them out of my own pocket, or I discounted their prices for the next services they received. I did not want to lose my clients and their bad service reflected on me. How many losses can one company take? As many as you can until you get it right. That is what I have learned. It is hard to trust people in business because you do not know how their business will affect yours. You do not want them to make your business look bad. I felt that was exactly what would have happened. My clients had to be compensated because I didn't want to lose them and they trusted me. When you have clients who trust you, that means a lot, and that is something no one should take lightly.

We were offset a little bit, but I think we gained a few good customers and we still have a few of those today. The partnerships to me were not profitable. Maybe I should say, the businesses we partnered with did not really work for me. Be careful who you partner with. My whole vision for every one of my clients is to help them get a little further, with their refund goals in mind. If it isn't going to go for a car, maybe it is for a mortgage. Maybe you can start your own business with your refund.

The thought of helping other businesses rang in my head so hard that I began to lease some of the extra offices I had to help some of the business owners in my circle have their own office space. These businesses would still be centered around what people liked to do with their refund. One was a travel service and the other was a graphic design business. These two businesses would receive traffic from some of my already-established clients and vice versa. These partnerships were firm, and I liked the way we tried to advertise and work together on different projects.

We spent a whole year together, until we got new neighbors in the space across from us. These people were loud and disrespectful, and their clients hung out on the outside. It was very distracting because they were always loud somehow, either yelling or with the music. It made a lot of other businesses in the plaza uncomfortable, and with the company they kept, it made it hard for our customers to park. This was happening during the off-season, but I began to worry about how my clients would be offended or would be very uncomfortable. One business decided to leave and put in their notice. They complained that this disturbance pushed away clients, and it made our area look bad and rundown.

Once again, I was in a terrible spot, but this time I went to the landlord and complained. These two landlords were like good cop/bad cop. The good landlord, who was white, told me the bad landlord, who was from another country, knew these people and was trying to help them out. The bad landlord told me there was nothing he could do and I should be happy because it would bring me more clients. I even had a client who was a social worker scared to get out of her car to enter my office due to the ranting and raving in the parking lot.

How does your business represent itself? Do you think your business is loud and obnoxious? How can other businesses around you maintain their clientele with loud and disrespectful people coming in and out of your business? I hope that is not you.

One of my tenants who rented an office from me asked me, "Can't you do anything about all this?"

I spoke with the good cop landlord and asked if there was anything he suggested. He offered me another space at a different plaza, but the rent was double what we were paying. The space use to be a dentist's office and it was filled with even more offices. I took the offer, thinking the three of us would go in together, looking forward to more spaces to help other businesses, but the travel agency fell off. The decision was not unanimous, as I had expected. It hurt me for a while. This was someone whom I had groomed for business and helped as a mentor. However, this move would go on without that person.

We went in, fixing and improving the office space. A lot had not been done. The ideas for the place had us with high hopes. We even had a large kitchen and conference room if we decided to hold events. We could have many uses for this space. After we moved in, I met a mortgage officer, Illiyah, who was a few offices down from us. Right off, we began to network and help one another with referrals. As my clientele and networks now began to come together, along with the other services we provided, the problems began to come in.

Chapter 8

Division

It was December of 2016, and by that time we had three other tenants occupying spaces within our office. Training had begun, marketing had taken off due to I was finally able to borrow the money from a financial institution, and at the same time. I linked up with a few people for commercials, billboards, and my tenant who I had knew previously was my graphic design guy had updated all my materials on the business to a look which represented us much better than in the past. We had over seven employees, and Amy and Danielle still were my LEAD people.

The relationship I had with a new guy was going well. I had decided to date once again. I guess I had no quarrels at the time, but people had begun telling me he was just not my type. I guess they were looking for someone from my professional life, or who represented that at least. This guy was sort of street and was just beginning a new life, or beginning to create his own journey. A lot of people judged us off the top. He continued to help me with many of the tasks I was trying to get done, tasks like getting the flyers out, social media advertising, and equipment and supply runs. We started an employment agency to better help our clients with jobs, but that was taking off slowly.

The tax season came in and the office was busy. We had upgraded to transferring phone lines and extensions, new software that linked us all, a mobile app for clients who couldn't get out, more clients who needed business help, plenty of space to park, and finally, we had signage. We were finally branded at all levels. I could finally call my company a corporation.

All my clients were satisfied and that made me undeniably happy, but when March came, Amy dropped a bomb on me: she was ready to leave Milwaukee. It hurt a lot, but she kept assuring me everything would work out. She was leaving her clients in good hands, she said. I smiled about it, but in the back of my head, I knew some of them might leave. Amy was unique and what she had come to do with me was completed. She was ready for new beginnings.

Not long after that, Danielle began to investigate her own space for her businesses. She had two: the payroll business and a nail shop. I could not be mad at either one of them. They both had played a major role in the company. They both told me, no matter what, they were just a call away.

After tax season, a new tenant came aboard and more changes began to happen. The only thing that stayed consistent was Illiyah, the mortgage guy who continued to send me clients all year long. I began to build a relationship with him as a networking business. The clients he sent were of a different caliber and were appreciated because those referrals helped my business to stay afloat during the off-season. Most of them were businessmen and women, and with that, I began to service them more than once.

Then, one of my clients came in with a huge problem that showed me that most people still don't want to do right by themselves or by you. He had employees but did not render payroll. He was paying his employees in cash. He had not told me anything when he brought me papers showing he was being audited. I did not know how to begin to help him, but a call from the State Unemployment Division helped me quickly. He had told them I knew everything; just contact her. WOW! I mean, can you say, thrown under the bus? I had no clue what was going on. I had been thrown in the deep end and had to swim out!

A call to Danielle helped me with this one, especially the payroll. Once we dissected the situation, he had a payroll lady, but she wasn't speaking to him. It took us a minute to talk her into helping us get his information to undo what had been done. It was crazy. How did we get involved in someone else's mess? That is exactly how people will do. As I have repeatedly stated, my job is service. I began to get to the State all the documents they were asking for, only to realize that nothing had been done correctly or either had not been done at all. Both Danielle and I had to help generate reports of who were employees, their pay, and whether they were an employee or a contractor. This was a huge thing for the State, because if they considered those people "employees", he would owe them a substantial amount of unemployment compensation.

Once we got to the end of the audit, we found out he was not going to owe as much as we had thought, but the agent turned to me and said, "Now you!"

I was like, "Who, me?"

"Yes, you. You are the person he said had his books, so we want to see yours."

Can you imagine how I felt, having been thrown into the middle of something of which I had absolutely no knowledge? These are the types of things you must be ready for in business. One thing for sure is, have all of your paperwork ready and current.

The quest the agent was on was easy for me and I did not hesitate to submit everything he needed. This is the way I want all my clients to be. I assured the agent that my client would not disregard the employee vs. contractor distinction again because we would be taking over his situation by giving him some employees through our employee agency and the agent was pleased. But that did not work for my client. He had many questions on how I was going to profit from it. After all the help I had been to him, even after he had thrown me under the bus, I still seemed like small cheese to him. All I could do was go ahead and bill him for my services rendered during the audit.

We were back again to people not working together. We were working too hard to not be valued. The customer made sure to take a long time to pay his outstanding invoice, which hurt all of us who had been part of the project. We wanted to get paid. Unfortunately, when he did come in to pay, he showed little respect for me and told me I never told him how nice he looked! I guess that was the beginning of the end of that client and I doing business. On his way out, he ran into my new boyfriend I told you about and they had a little disagreement in the parking lot. That was icing on the cake. He made sure he mentioned the situation everywhere he went.

Even though I'd told my boyfriend not to interfere in my situations, he never listened. He had even told my tenants they were unfair by not paying their rent on time and that it made me suffer personally trying to uphold the rent until they could pay. I call it the mudslide effect. One thing goes bad, then everything after begins to slide off as well. Two tenants moved out and one never showed up again. There was only one left.

We did the best we could to keep going until we just could not hold on any longer. That one tenant, I really loved her loyalty. It brought me peace knowing I had done everyone right. They others just wanted special treatment. She even mentioned that her husband would have stood in and said something too. It was unfair to continue to not do good business.

Chapter 9

When The Going Gets Tough

After all the tenants had left, we could no longer hold up paying the rent. After a few months, I had sacrificed everything I had. I had to change my residence due to the strain it had caused. Waiting on the new place, I was in limbo: no place to call home for thirty days. I let my girls stay with my oldest daughter. My boyfriend and I slept in the big office where we still were leasing. I thought back to my mom and dad, and how they'd had us sleep in their shop that one time. I smiled to myself and said, "Wow. I've made it. If you can sacrifice everything for your vision, you have arrived at a place where nothing will stop you."

For those next few weeks, our church needed somewhere to hold services until their work on the church was done. They paid me to have services in my office every Sunday. I called it a blessing. Visions Tax was receiving the anointing it needed to move on. A month later, I was offered a business loan from my bank. I was able to move my residence and move my business. Once again, we relocated.

My then-boyfriend and his friends moved my business to a small suite close to malls and other larger businesses. I began to believe I could do no more than I was doing, that I wasn't going to grow or expand any further than where I was. The business was staying at the same level and there was no increase. I told myself

I would concentrate only on me and my family. The ideas and other services I would do at a minimum.

I focused more on stories I wanted to tell about what has happened in my life. I published a book about my young life that I had written many years ago when I was with my first husband. I felt good that I was checking off things I'd always wanted to accomplish. I'm not saying, go out there and become an author. I'm just saying, sometimes you only find yourself caring about your well-being after you see what happens when you spend so much time caring for others. Is that selfish? No! I had given so much of myself for others to be great, financially free, and to lessen their burdens. I needed to lessen my burdens somehow too.

The new location was quite small, and it was probably the smallest space I had ever rented, but the area was upscale, and my clients felt safe discussing their monetary decisions. I became a business coach for a lot of the small businesses, and I trained my middle daughter to help me sort, separate, and total receipts. Even though we were steadily maintaining the business, I felt we still were missing something. I knew Visions Tax should have easily been able to double the clientele.

We started a new referral program, which clients jumped on, that helped us to bring in new clientele, but the main person who referred the most clients was still Illiyah. I liked that the top-referring clients received our appreciation with gifts and certificates, but I was still discouraged that our service was not at the top, where I felt after all these years we should have been. We had not doubled our clientele; it always stayed in the same numbers, year after year.

In my thirteenth year of tax season, I decreased everything, taking down my overhead to a minimum. I began to want to save so I could expand the business. We dropped down to one employee and one preparer, which was me, and we just worked until our fingers fell off. I began to let people close to me know I was leaving. I needed to expand Visions Tax and look for new clientele, and at the same time, promote all my other services. I had looked at Georgia because I knew there was a lot of competition, but at the same time, I was only looking to double the clientele. I wanted to spread Visions Tax out to people who had never heard of us because I knew there were people out there who needed us.

Chapter 10

Bust The Move: Your Comeback

Anything that grows must go through a series of changes...

~ Pastor JP

My transition to Georgia led me on a journey to see people in business another way. It also made me speak up, stand up, and talk more about my business. I was shy and hesitant about getting up in front of people, but going to a place where no one knows you, all you can do is deliver. To my surprise, people were a lot like me and had similar goals and dreams. People were embracing one another, and there were women holding group meetings to help each other achieve branding. It reminded me of the movie, *Malcom X*, where Malcolm went overseas and found people just like him.

My first event was a Women's Expo, and it was huge. There were women from all around, women of all types of cultures and businesses. Not one bad look or attitude was amongst us, just people excited about what you had to offer. That opened the door to many other events and get-togethers. I met a lot of people in businesses which moved me into a place where I was hungry to be known. I only wanted people to understand my services and why I'd come to help. The women I networked with were strong and we met every Wednesday. Before long, my first book was in the bookstore near where I lived, and my Georgia clientele began to embrace me. I had started a new location by December 2019 and began to go to work.

I'd thought I would lose my clients in Milwaukee because they had heard I moved, but to my surprise they hung in there while I made the transition. If you have a great service, you should not worry much about losing people, but get ready for the new clients and the increase. We cannot look backwards to what we did wrong or what we did right; we must learn from the good *and* the bad, so we can make better decisions in our business.

I now had a few employees, and not only did we maintain our clientele, we increased it. Still today, Illiyah is the number-one business for referring business to me, and that partnership has taught me so much about what a networking partnership should consist of. If you have a partnering business, you want to make sure they operate similar to the way you do, meaning they do business and service clients in a manner like you do. That is what makes your clients happy.

It may be okay to lose people along the way, but remember, it is about your transition and your service. "We are a seed that was planted with a purpose," a quote from Pastor JP.

My clients have no problems referring us to anyone now, and most new clients say all roads point to Visions Tax when they ask for good services.

We are now heading toward fifteen years in service this year. How many of you know a business that has lasted that long? The Road to Entrepreneurship takes a lot of work to execute in order for it to come together. It will not come overnight, but your endurance will cause you to win if you keep on choo-choo-chooing...